FROM THE KITCHEN
TO THE TABLE
IN 10 MINUTES
3 STEPS and You're Done!

27 RECIPES CREATED WITH THE HELP OF
THE ALÍCIA FOUNDATION

First edition: September 2013

© Lékué, 2012

© Editorial Amat, 2012 (www.amateditorial.com) [Amat Publishing House]
   Profit Editorial I., S.L. Barcelona, 2012

Cookbook Reference: LIB00024

Recipes: Alícia Foundation with contributing USA recipe developer Karla Senior

Original idea and coordination: Lékué, www.lekuecooking.com

Nutritional information: Alícia Foundation

Art and Design Direction: Nomon Design

Photo credits: Javier Mendiola

Chef: Amanda Laporte

ISBN: 978-84-616-5670-7

Legal deposit: B. 20924-2013

Printing: Ferrercoll

Printed in Spain

FROM THE KITCHEN
TO THE TABLE
IN 10 MINUTES

3 STEPS and You're Done!

27 RECIPES CREATED WITH THE HELP OF
THE ALÍCIA FOUNDATION

CONTENTS

Lékué introduction

We can all think of those traditional recipes (Spanish omelets, roasted vegetables, fish, meat, sponge cakes, etc.), however, many of us don't know the easiest way to make them or simply get overwhelmed by the thought of how much time it would take us to cook them. That's why we are constantly looking for alternatives that meet our needs, help us improve our quality of life and, particularly, **that promote a healthy diet.**

Experience tells us that when cooking it is just as important what we make as how we make it. Along these lines, we and the Alícia Foundation share one common goal for this new edition: "**to help us all eat better**".

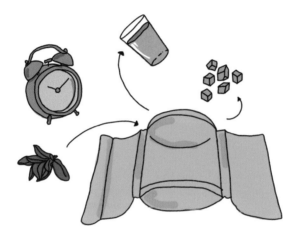

A complete team of cooking professionals has prepared this new cookbook to help you cook fast, clean, safe, and healthy meals; recipes that pamper each and every food while it is cooked in the microwave so as to allow us to enjoy the ingredients original flavors in a different way. **In just 10 minutes you can add a vegetable lasagna or potato gratin to your weekly menu.**

In order to make cooking easier than ever, **this book includes 27 simple microwave cooking recipes that you can mix and match following the recommended weekly nutritional guidelines.** Each recipe also comes with tips and tricks to help you achieve the desired result and will also tell you the amount of the 3 food groups in the meals that you will make using each recipe.

At Lékué and the Alícia Foundation we have worked to provide recipes adapted to today's times. In doing so we have worked with the best cooks, chemists, food technologists, nutritionists and designers, all working toward the same goal: to make cooking a gastronomic experience that will captivate the palate of all those who are starting to learn how to cook and those who, while not forgetting about keeping a proper diet, value their time.

A well-equipped kitchen

In order to make your day-to-day recipes you will need some basic items in your kitchen that you simply cannot do without. With very few items you can create healthy menus that are fast and affordable to make. You don't need to have many utensils to enjoy cooking. All you'll need is:

- **Silverware**: It is important to have knives, spoons and forks. A well-sharpened knife makes cooking a lot easier.

- **Cutting boards**: That are strong and easy to wash. Remember to use a different board for each food group: meat, fish or vegetables. You can use a different colored board for each food group or clean them after each use.

- A **bowl**: For making our mixtures.

- A **whisk**, **slotted spoon**, and **spatula**.

- A **steam case**: For cooking fish, meat, vegetables, etc., or an **Ogya** for cooking foods with greater volume such as sauces or soups.

- **Storage containers**: It is essential to have containers that allow you to properly store foods, whether in the refrigerator or freezer.

- Other recommended utensils: **brushes**, **spatulas**, etc.

Once equipped but before starting to cook we must make a basic kit of essential ingredients. Here's **your first shopping list:**

These are some ingredients that should be staples in your pantry, that way you have them on hand whenever you need them:

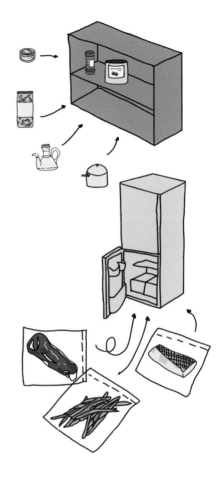

- Legumes: chickpeas, lentils, cooked beans.

- Nuts: almonds, toasted hazelnuts, walnuts, peanuts, etc.

- Olive oil: extra virgin, if possible, which has more aroma and is healthier.

- Sauces and condiments: salt, vinegar, soy sauce, mustard, mayonnaise, and tomato sauce.

- Basic dried herbs and spices: pepper, paprika, nutmeg, curry, oregano, basil and Provençal-style herbs.

- Sugary goods: chocolate, jelly, honey and sugar.

- Canned goods: tomate frito (pureed tomato sauce), tuna and sardines.

For the freezer:

- Vegetables: spinach, peas, beans, stir-fry veggies, and chopped garlic and parsley.

- Meats: chicken, turkey, hamburgers, pork loin, sausage and steak.

- Fish: Salmon, sea bass, halibut, sole, striped bass.

- Broths, sauces and creams.

Remember that everything must be kept in closed containers made for preventing foods from perishing or acquiring an unpleasant odor.

The maximum amount of time we can keep a **fresh product that we have frozen is three months**. It is also very important not to defrost frozen products at room temperature (it is always better to do so in the refrigerator) and make sure that the food has reached a high enough temperature when reheating.

Follow the recipes in the book or let your imagination run wild. At home, feel totally free to experiment with new combinations, cooking times and adventurous ways of serving your dishes! Little by little, you'll find out what works and train your **mental palate** until one day you are able to create new dishes and know if they'll be popular without even trying them. **When cooking, prohibitions are prohibited!**

Smart Grocery Shopping

Shopping is a very important part of cooking. In fact, we actually start cooking at the time we go shopping and therefore the end result of our dishes will depend largely on our shopping skills.

Here are some useful tips for grocery shopping and getting the best produce:

Fruits and vegetables:

- Always pay attention to the origin and seasonality of the product, as it will provide you have better-tasting fruits and vegetables and you'll save up on your purchase.

- Don't trust in perfect looking fruits and vegetables:

  - Look for apples with those slight streaked spots near the stem.

  - Choose bananas with tiny black dots. Those ones are very sweet.

  - Pears with little brown spots are juicier and softer.

  - Look for tangerines and oranges that still have their leaves, as this indicates that the fruit is fresh.

  - Small zucchinis have the most flavor because they have less water.

  - Lettuce with more green leaves (romaine, butter-head, etc.) has more vitamin C.

- Tricks for large items:

  - Melon: Press using your thumbs on both sides, the softer the riper.

  - Pineapple: Tug on one of the top leaves and if it comes out easily, it is ready to use.

Fish:

How do I determine its quality?

  - Bulging, shiny eyes indicate that it is fresher.

  - For small fish (sardines, red mullet, young hake) make sure that they are hard and smooth, as this indicates they are the freshest.

- Ask about its origin. The closer it is to you, the fresher and more sustainable it will be. Ask the person in charge where you buy your fish. They will be your best teacher.

Meat:

- If possible, buy shiny, brightly colored meats rather than dull, dark ones.
- Ask the butcher to grind meat for hamburgers. They will be fresher and you can choose the part you want.
- When buying packaged meat, pay attention to its price by weight. The more preparation/storage/packaging procedures involved (sliced, cut, breaded, etc.) the more costly it will be.
- For beef, pieces that have more fat scattered throughout the meat will be softer. Careful not to get this confused with the meat nerves!

Lastly, here is an overview of the dos and don'ts of good grocery shopping:

1. **It is not recommended to go grocery shopping when you are hungry:** In order to avoid temptations.
2. **Plan your meals:** Don't let yourself get carried away by impulses and think before you buy.
3. **The shopping list, your cheat sheet for the exam:** Write down all the products you need.
4. **Get familiar with the layout of products in the market or supermarket:** Get the heaviest items first and the frozen items at the end. Just as in prehistoric times, when you go out to get food you have to be agile and stay alert. You'll get your chance to take a stroll when you go to the mall!
5. **Use the Internet:** It's convenient, it saves you time and it enables you to compare prices.
6. **Compare prices:** Pay attention to each price of the produce by weight.
7. **It's a good idea to buy fresh products:** Which are local and seasonal.
8. **Always have your must-haves on hand:** So that your pantry is never missing the basics.
9. **Sustainable shopping:** Avoid unnecessary packaging, buy loose produce whenever possible and pay attention to their origin.
10. **Enjoy the market and specialized stores:** Talk to the shopkeepers and ask them to get your meat or fish ready for cooking.

Cooking and microwave tricks

When microwave cooking, using a steam case is very handy and it can come in handy to learn some essential tricks for making your dishes even more appealing:

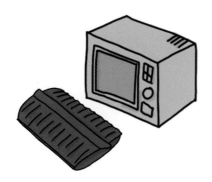

Cooking meat and fish:

- Cooking times are very short. This is because their main component, protein, is very sensitive to changes in temperature and cooks very quickly.

- We recommend not to extend the cooking times. Instead, let it sit for a minute with the case closed. (See table on page 16 for cooking times).

- Use the rack with 2-3 tablespoons of water underneath to help moisten the fish and meat without soaking them in the cooking water. You can also add rosemary or Provençal-style herbs for seasoning.

- You can also cook meat with sauces without the rack, which will help us make them more tender.

General tips:

- The steam case will help us make the temperature uniform thanks to the steam effect that is created inside. This helps to keep the food more moist and juicy.

- Cooking on the edges of the case is more intense than in the middle, so try to put the thickest parts of the food on the outside and the thinnest parts in the middle.

- In general it isn't necessary to add oil for cooking. You can add it raw at the end or, if you prefer, you can do so while cooking to give your dish an added flavor.

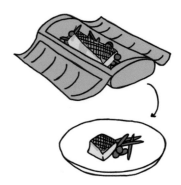

Cooking fruits and vegetables:

- The fibers in fruits and vegetables make their cooking times longer than those of meat and fish in general seeing that higher temperatures are needed to break them down.

- Add 2-3 tablespoons of water to vegetables before beginning to cook them as this will help keep them moist.

- The final color of vegetables cooked in the microwave is more intense than when cooked by traditional boiling. That doesn't mean that they are less cooked, it is just that this type of cooking leads to less loss of color, vitamins and minerals.

Microwave. RememBer!

- **Every microwave is different;** check the cooking time for the product and add more time to taste if you feel it isn't cooked enough yet.

- When using the 3 – 4 person Lékué Steam Case with tray, cooking time increases...for doubling the amount, calculate double time minus one or two minutes.

- If you have a frozen product, you can defrost it first in the same case with the defrosting program in your microwave or at minimum power, and then follow the times provided.

Oven. RememBer!

- **Not all foods cook at the same temperature due to their different makeup.**

- Cooking time does not increase with the amount of food. For example: one potato and two potatoes have the same cooking time.

- Due to this kind of cooking, cooking times are longer than in the microwave.

Food	Recommendation	Amount	Microwave (800 W)	Rest Time	Oven (°F/time)
Vegetables and starches					
Artichokes (heads)	2 tbsp water	2 units	4'		355° F, 45'
Asparagus	1 tbsp water	4 oz	4'		355° F, 25'
Bell Pepper	1 tbsp water	4 oz	4'		355° F, 30'
Broccoli	2 tbsp water	4 oz	3'		355° F, 45'
Carrots	2 tbsp water	4 oz	3'		355° F, 35'
Eggplant	1 tbsp water	4 oz	4'		355° F, 45'
Frozen Peas	cook frozen	4 oz	3'		355° F, 25'
Green Beans	2 tbsp water	4 oz	4'		355° F, 35'
Leeks	1 tbsp water + 1 tbsp oil	1 unit	6'		355° F, 40'
Mushrooms	use tray	4 oz	2'		355° F, 30'
Onion (sauce base)	1 tbsp water + 1 tbsp oil	1.5 oz	3'		355° F, 30'
Potato (half)	4 tbsp water	1 medium unit	9'		355° F, 45'
Tomato (half)	-	1 medium unit	1' 30"		355° F, 30'
Zucchini	2 tbsp water	4 oz	7'		355° F, 30'
Seafood					
Bass	Tray with 2 tbsp water	4.5 oz	1' 30"	1'	320° F, 15'
Clams	Tray with 2 tbsp water	5 oz	2'		320° F, 30'
Hake	Tray with 2 tbsp water	4.5 oz	1' 30"	1'	320° F, 15'
Halibut	Tray with 2 tbsp water	5 oz	2'	1'	320° F, 20'
Mackerel	Tray with 2 tbsp water	4.5 oz	2'	1'	320° F, 15'
Salmon	Tray with 2 tbsp water	4.5 oz	1' 30"	1'	320° F, 15'
Shrimp	Tray with 2 tbsp water	6 units	2'		320° F, 20'
Sole (fillets)	Tray with 2 tbsp water	4.5 oz	1' 30"	1'	320° F, 10'
Squid	Tray with 2 tbsp water	1 unit	2'		320° F, 30'
Meat					
Beef Strips	Tray with 2 tbsp water	4 oz	2'	30"	355° F, 20'
Chicken Thigh	Tray with 2 tbsp water	4 oz	2'	30"	355° F, 45'
Hamburger	Tray with 2 tbsp water	4 oz	2'	30"	355° F, 20'
Pork	Tray with 2 tbsp water	4 oz	2'	30"	355° F, 15'
Sausage	Tray with 2 tbsp water	1 link	2'	30"	355° F, 40'
Turkey Breast	Tray with 2 tbsp water	4 oz	2'	30"	255° F, 20'
Fruit					
Apple	Quartered	1 unit	3'		355° F, 25'
Figs	Halved with tray	2 units	1'30"		355° F, 30'
Pear	Diced	1 unit	3'		355° F, 25'
Pineapple	sliced	1 1" round slice	4"		355° F, 40'

What is platinum silicone?

Platinum silicone is a type of silicone that uses platinum (precious metal) as a binding agent, making it completely odorless, anti-bacteria and **resistant to high and low temperatures.**

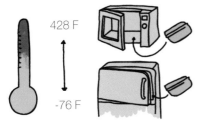

428 F

-76 F

That is why it is perfect and absolutely safe for its use in hospital, surgical material, prostheses, medical implants and **baby bottle teats.**

Because it does not alter the flavor of foods, or leave any kind of residue, it is also ideal for making moulds and utensils that come into contact with food, like Lékué products.

In addition, its non-stick properties ensure **removing food from the mould is easy**. There is no need to grease the moulds, thus eliminating the excessive use of butter and/or oils ensuring healthier, non-fat cooking.

As a commitment to safety, Lékué applies strict quality controls, guaranteeing a perfect end product. In addition, after the manufacturing process is completed, all Lékué products go through a curing process in the oven for 4 hours at 215°C/419°F to eliminate any possible residues, so **you can relax and enjoy your food.**

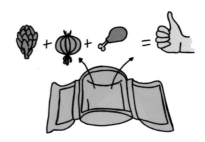

Nutrition section outline

Eating well means eating everything in a **balanced** and **varied** way that is **adapted** to each individual according to their culinary culture and tradition.

It is important not to leave long gaps between food intakes throughout the day. **It is recommended to eat five meals a day.**

We often forget one of the most important meals, the one that helps us start our day: **Breakfast**.

For a healthy diet, remember to follow the magical triangle, as follows:

During **meals** and **dinner** don't forget to always include foods from all the three groups in your meals. Below, there is a visual that shows you which foods are essential for your daily menu::

Have in mind!

To eat everything from all the food groups, but not all in the same amount. *For example: if you are going to play sports, it will burn a lot more energy, thus eat a greater amount of carbohydrates. On the other hand, if you want to have a low-fat meal, eat a larger proportion of vegetables.*

V = Vegetables

C = Carbohydrates
Starchy food (pasta, rice, potatoes, legumes, etc.)

P = Protein
(Meat, fish, eggs, legumes, etc.)

*Drink plenty of water. For cooking and seasoning, use olive oil. For dessert, have some fruit or occasionally a dairy product.

Afternoon snacks are a great wild card for us to complete our daily recommended intake: a piece of fruit in case we still haven't had any throughout the day; a dairy product adds up to our daily intake of that particular food group part, and a sandwich is a great call if we've used up lots of energy during the day, etc.

This table summarizes and helps us remember the number of servings to be eaten daily:

Healthy diet

Fruits	3-3.5 servings/day
Vegetables	2 servings/day
Legumes	2-4 servings/week
Dairy	2-3 servings/day
Meat	3-4 servings/week
Fish	3-4 servings/week
Oily fish	1-2 servings/week
Eggs	3-4 servings/week
Fried foods	2-3 times/week
Soft drinks, juices	2-3 items/week
Baked goods, pastries and snacks	2-3 items/week

Have in mind!

Also remember that you should be physically active every day as this gives you great benefits both at a physical and psychological level.

Vegetables and Legumes

Vegetable

Mushroom Pizzas

Ingredients

 8 baby bella mushrooms

 4 tbsp canned crushed tomatoes

Grated mozzarella cheese

1 tbsp water

 Oregano

 Salt and pepper

1/4 tsp sugar

Directions

❶ Wash the mushrooms and remove the stems. Add water to the Lékué Steam Case and place tray inside. Place the mushrooms on top of the tray in the Lékué Steam Case.

❷ In a small bowl, mix the crushed tomatoes, sugar, a pinch of salt, and a pinch of pepper. Fill the mushrooms with the tomato mixture and sprinkle dried oregano on top. Put a pinch of mozzarella on each mushroom.

❸ Close the case and microwave for 3 minutes at maximum power (800 W).

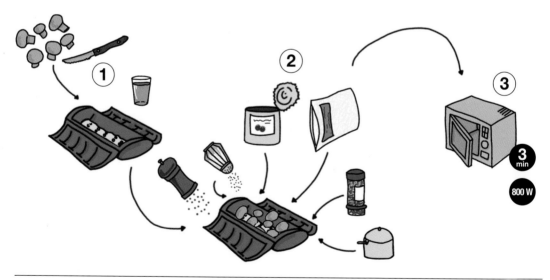

Tips and tricks

- *If you prefer you can add raw olive oil to give the dish more flavor.*
- *If you don't have crushed tomatoes you can also use tomato frito (pureed tomato sauce).*

Roasted Figs with Melted Goat Cheese

Ingredients

 4 small figs (5.5 oz., 160 g)

 1 **tsp** granulated sugar

1/4 - 1/3 cup crumbled goat cheese

Salad greens

Directions

❶ Cut the figs in half lengthwise and place them face up on the tray in the Lékué Steam Case, sprinkle with sugar, and cook for 2 minutes at 800 watts. (After 2 minutes, check the figs by poking them with a fork. If the figs are slightly larger, put them back in the microwave for 30 second increments. You shouldn't need to cook them longer than an additional minute.)

❷ Open the case and put the crumbled goat cheese on top of each fig. Close the lids again and cook for 1 more minute (800 W).

❸ Prepare a mixture of lettuce, arugula, and top with figs.

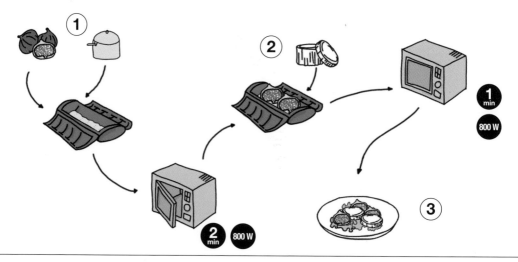

Tips and tricks

- *Serve with extra virgin olive oil vinaigrette, balsamic vinegar and toasted pine nuts. Best served hot!*
- *If you don't have goat cheese you can also use Brie or any other soft cheese.*

Vegetable

Vegetable Skewers

Ingredients

 1/3 cup sugar snap peas

 1/3 medium zucchini

 1/3 medium red bell pepper

 Salt

 2 tsp water

 2 wooden skewers

Directions

❶ Prep the vegetables by washing the snap peas. Cut the zucchini lengthwise down the center and then cut into 1/2 inch pieces. Season the vegetables with a couple pinches of salt and/or any other spices desired. Thread vegetables onto the skewers however you prefer.

❷ Add water to the Lékué Steam Case, and place tray in the case with the skewers.

❸ Close the lids and cook in the microwave for 4 minutes (800 W).

Tips and tricks

- If you are serving the skewers as an appetizer, combine them with whatever sauces you like. Here are some ideas for sauces that you can make cold by simply mixing their ingredients:

• *Paprika cheese:* 2 tablespoons soft cheese, 1 tablespoon olive oil and paprika.
• *Japanese sauce:* 2 tablespoons mayonnaise and 1 tablespoon soy sauce.
• *Alla diavola:* 2 tablespoons sofrito, a touch of tabasco and a pinch of dry thyme.
• *Rosemary alioli:* 2 tablespoons alioli and a pinch of rosemary.
• *Curry:* 2 tablespoons Greek yogurt and 1 tablespoon curry.

Vegetable

Asparagus with Prosciutto

Ingredients

 12 asparagus

 4 thick slices of prosciutto

1 tbsp water

Salt

Egg (optional)

Directions

❶ Remove about an inch from the ends of the asparagus. Place 3 asparagus together and roll 1 piece of prosciutto around the bunch in the center. Continue with the remaining asparagus.

❷ Place the rolled asparagus in the Lékué Steam Case and add the water and a pinch of salt. Close the lids and cook in the microwave for 4 minutes at 800 watts.

❸ Remove the case and enjoy. If desired you can simply add an egg to the dish by cracking an egg into the steam case, and then cooking again for an additional minute.

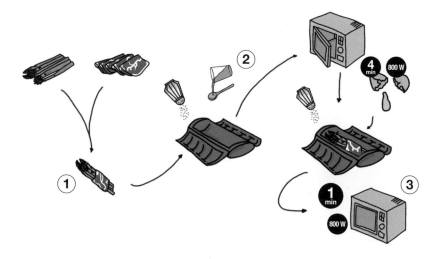

Tips and tricks

- Cooking time for the egg varies according to taste. Add a few seconds if it doesn't seem cooked enough.
- Remember that eggs give us high-quality proteins, vitamins (A, D and B12) and minerals. Consuming 3 or 4 eggs per week is a good alternative to meat and fish.
- You can use Serrano, Iberian, or York ham or plain turkey breast.

Vegetable

Tomato with Tuna Salad

Ingredients

 1 tomato, halved and seeded

 2 tbsp water

 1 can of tuna, drained

 Salad Greens, your choice

 Red pepper flakes (optional)

 1 tbsp mayonnaise

 Salt and pepper

Directions

❶ Prep the tomato. Add the water to the Lékué Steam Case and place the rack inside.

❷ Place the tomato face up on the rack. Drizzle 1 tsp of olive oil over the tomato, and season with a pinch of salt and pepper. Close the lids and cook in the microwave for 2 minutes and 30 seconds at 800 watts.

❸ In the meantime, prepare the tuna salad. In a separate bowl mix the canned, drained tuna, mayonnaise, pinch of salt and pepper, and red pepper flakes. Remove the steam case from the microwave and open the lids. Arrange a bed of lettuce on a plate and stuff the slightly cooled tomatoes with the tuna salad. Place the stuffed tomatoes on top of the lettuce.

Tips and tricks

- *You can also make this recipe in the Ogya.*
- *You can also add olives, anchovies, capers, pickles, chopped parsley or chopped hard-boiled egg.*
- *You can make the mayonnaise at home. For this you'll need 1 egg and about 2/3 cup (150 ml) of oil. Put the egg in a tall container and add the oil bit by bit while blending with the mixer until it makes an emulsion. Lastly, add a pinch of salt to taste.*
- *If desired, you can make egg-free mayonnaise with 3 cups of oil and 1 cup of milk. Mix the ingredients and blend with the mixer from the bottom up until making an emulsion.*

Vegetable

Potato Gratin

Ingredients

 1 large potato

 3/4 cup cream

 1 egg yolk

 Salt

 Pepper

 1/4 cup Gruyere cheese

Directions

❶ Peel and slice the potato. In a separate bowl mix the egg yolk and cream together. Now add the grated Gruyere and a pinch of salt and pepper.

❷ Put a layer of potatoes in the Lékué Steam Case and then a layer of the cream mixture. Repeat this process until the steam case is full. Add one more pinch of salt and pepper to the top.

❸ Close the lids and cook in the microwave for 10 minutes at 800 watts.

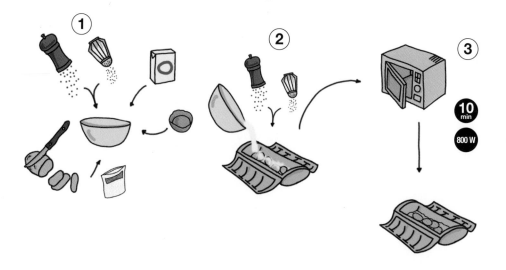

Tips and tricks

- You can include fillets of anchovies, (boiled) ham or bacon interspersed between the potato slices to give it added flavor.
- Don't worry if the edges come out a tan color – it is just the cream being cooked. This has a great flavor.

Vegetable

Peas with Onions and Bacon

Ingredients

🧅 **1/2 small** yellow onion

🥓 **2 strips** of bacon, diced

🟢 **3/4 - 1 cup** frozen peas

🧂 Pepper

🪣 **2 tbsp** water

🧂 Salt

Directions

❶ Put the diced bacon into the Lékué Steam Case with a pinch of pepper. Close the lids and cook for 2 minutes at 800 watts.

❷ Add the chopped onion to the case along with 1 tbsp water and a pinch of pepper. Cook again for another 2 minutes at 800 watts.

❸ Add the peas, 1 tbsp water and another pinch of salt and pepper. Close the lids and cook for 3 minutes at 800 watts.

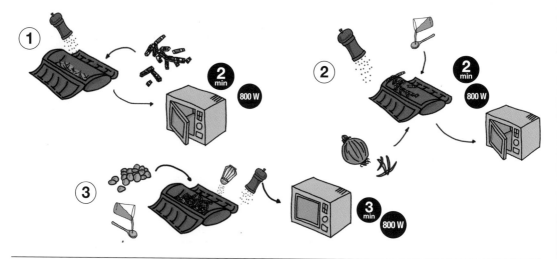

Tips and tricks

- If you have white wine, use it instead of water. Your dish will turn out even more delicious. Another trick? Sprinkle with aniseed on top and stir immediately after taking it out of the microwave.
- If you crush it well with a mixer while adding a bit of water, you'll get delicious warm creamed peas.
- If using canned peas, shorten the cooking time in step 3 to 1 minute.
- Try adding a pinch of cinnamon, as this will give it a very special touch.
- If you have a mint plant you can add a few leaves after taking it out of the microwave.

Leeks in Roquefort Cream

Ingredients

 3 medium leeks

 1/4 cup cream

 1/4 cup milk

 1/4 cup Roquefort cheese

 Salt

Directions

❶ Remove the outer layer of the leeks and wash off any dirt. Trim the root and most of the green tops from the leeks. Cut each leek into 3 pieces.

❷ Put all ingredients into the Lékué Steam Case. Close the lids and cook in the microwave for 8 minutes at 800 watts. Remove the case from the microwave.

❸ Place the leeks on a serving dish and drizzle the sauce over top. Serve warm.

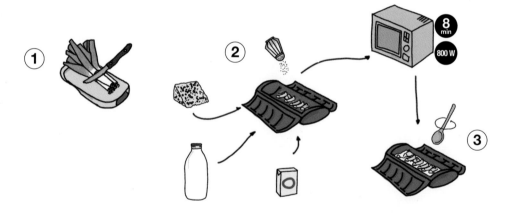

Tips and tricks

- If you have a little left over, chop the leeks with a knife and you'll have an excellent spaghetti sauce you can save for later by putting it in the freezer.
- Once it's done, if you find the taste stronger than you expected (because the sauce is too thick), you can simply pour in a little milk and it's good to go.
- Have in mind this is a high calorie dish, thanks to the cream and cheese. You should eat it only on certain occasions and balance it with the rest of your menu: meat or fish with a side salad.
- You don't have to use Roquefort cheese; any type of blue cheese can be substituted.

Lentils with Mixed Vegetables

Ingredients

 1/4 small white onion, diced

 1/4 cup red pepper, diced

 1/2 small carrot, diced

1 tbsp pureed tomato sauce

1 tbsp water

1 tbsp olive oil

Salt

Pepper

2/3 cup cooked lentils

Directions

❶ Cut the vegetables and place them in the Lékué Steam Case with tomato puree, water, olive oil, and a pinch of salt and pepper.

❷ Mix well, close the case and cook for 3 minutes at 800 watts.

❸ Add the cooked lentils, stir together, and cook for another minute.

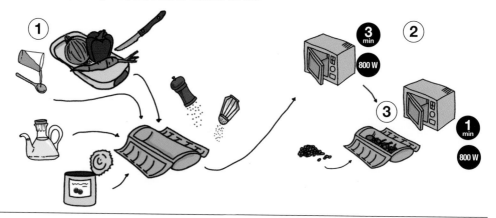

Tips and tricks

- You can also make this recipe in the Lékué Ogya.
- If desired, use whatever vegetables you have in the refrigerator to make this recipe.
- Have a bit of chorizo? Cut it into thin pieces and add it along with a teaspoon of hot paprika to make Rioja-style lentils.
- You can try variations of this recipe using chickpeas, beans, etc.
- Remember that lentils provide us with carbohydrates, proteins, fiber, vitamins and minerals. Combining lentils with rice will give you a source of better quality proteins.
- You can make lentils faster in the Lékué RiceCooker than on the stove. Just add 1 cup of dried lentils into the RiceCooker with 2 cups of water. Put it in the microwave and cook for 20 minutes at 800 watts.

Vegetable

Vegetable Lasagna

Ingredients

 Lasagna noodles (pre-cooked)

 1/3 zucchini

 1 1/4 cup crushed tomatoes

 1/2 small white onion

 1/4 eggplant

 1/3 red bell pepper

 Grated Parmesan cheese

 Salt

 Pepper

Directions

❶ Roughly chop the pepper and onion. Slice the zucchini and eggplant into 1/4 inch slices. Season the vegetables with a few pinches of salt and pepper. Start to assemble the lasagna by starting with a thin layer (about 1 tbsp) of crushed tomatoes on the bottom of the Lékué Steam Case.

❷ Next put a lasagna noodle on top and then some more crushed tomatoes. Layer half of the vegetables in any order you wish. Finish that layer with crushed tomatoes and a sprinkle of cheese. Add another noodle and continue with the other half of the vegetables. Top with sauce and a little more cheese. Finish the lasagna with a noodle, layer with tomatoes and cheese.

❸ Close the Lékué Steam Case and put in the microwave for 7 minutes at 800 watts. Remove from the microwave and enjoy.

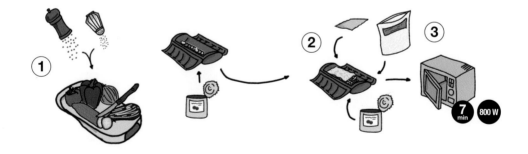

Tips and tricks

- If desired, you can use other vegetables such as carrots, mushrooms, green pepper, etc.
- You can use tomato frito instead of crushed tomatoes.
- Try using other cheeses such as Emmenthal, Grana Padano or cured Manchego cheeses.
- Add hazelnut slivers or raisins to the vegetables to give it a different or unexpected touch.
- This dish can be made with no boil lasagna noodles saving you time! If using no boil noodles, increase the time to 10 minutes and cut the zucchini and eggplant ½ inch thick because it will be cooking for a longer amount of time.

White Beans with Clams

Ingredients

 1/3 cup cooked white beans

 8 clams

 1 clove of garlic, chopped

2 tbsp fresh parsley, roughly chopped

 Salt

Pepper

1 tbsp water

Directions

❶ Put the beans, parsley, garlic, and clams into the Lékué Steam Case. Add the water, and a pinch of salt and pepper.

❷ Close the case and cook in the microwave for 3 minutes and 30 seconds at 800 watts.

❸ Remove from the microwave and check to see if all clams have opened. If they haven't, cook for an additional minute.

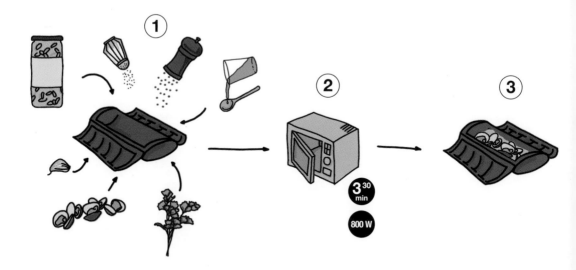

Tips and tricks

- *This dish could also be made in the Lékué Ogya.*
- *You can add raw oil at the end for added flavor.*
- *Try using fresh cockles instead of clams.*

Vegetable

Artichokes in Green Sauce

Ingredients

 1/3 cup water

 1 tsp flour

 2 tsp olive oil

1 clove of garlic, chopped

Fresh parsley

 2 medium artichokes

Salt

Directions

❶ Add water, oil, flour, garlic, and chopped parsley to the Lékué Steam Case. Close the lids and cook in the microwave for 1 minute and 30 seconds at 800 watts.

❷ Stir the sauce well to bind it. Peel the artichokes until you are left with the hearts and cut the hearts into 4 pieces. To peel the artichoke, start pulling off the outer leaves and cut the base off.

❸ Add the artichoke hearts to the case and cook for another 4 minutes at 800 watts. Open the case, and mix well. Serve the artichokes with the sauce on top.

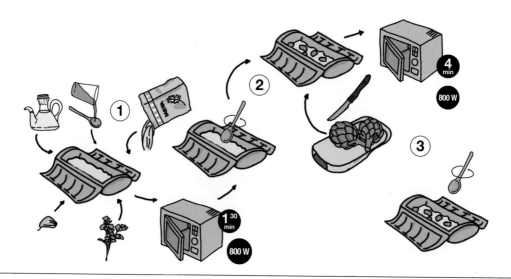

Tips and tricks

- You can also add drained canned asparagus or chopped hard-boiled egg when serving.

Fish

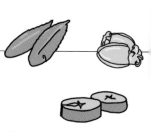

Fish

Sole with Capers and Lemons

Ingredients

 1 fillet of sole

 2 tbsp water

1 tbsp butter

Half of one lemon

1 tsp Capers

Fresh parsley

Salt

Olive oil

Directions

❶ Place the tray in the Lékué Steam Case. Add the water, sole, and a pinch of salt.

❷ Put the butter on top of the fish, along with a teaspoon of olive oil, capers and chopped parsley.

❸ Close the lids and cook in the microwave for 1 minute and 20 seconds at 800 watts. Leave the lids closed for another minute before serving. Spritz with Lékué Citrus Sprayer for added flavor.

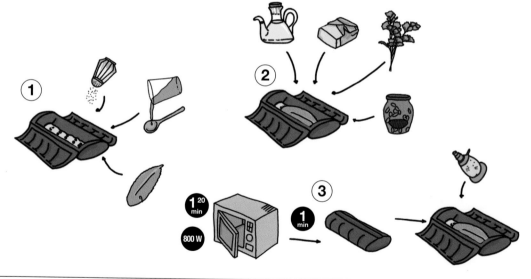

Tips and tricks

- Remember that it is very important to let it sit for one minute so that the fish can finish its cooking process with its own heat.

Fish

Halibut in White Wine

Ingredients

 1 tbsp water

 1 tbsp white wine

 1 tbsp wine vinegar

 1 sprig of rosemary

 1 - 5 oz Halibut fillet

 1 small carrot, peeled, cut into 1/4" rounds

 1/4 cup small yellow onion

 Lemon

 Salt and pepper

 Sugar

Directions

❶ Add the water, wine, vinegar, and rosemary to the Lékué Steam Case and place the tray inside.

❷ Cut the onion into strips and add to the Lékué Steam Case along with the carrot. Add the halibut. Sprinkle with a pinch of sugar, salt, and pepper and a squirt of lemon juice. Close the lids and cook for 2 minutes at 800 watts.

❸ Let sit for an additional minute before opening the case.

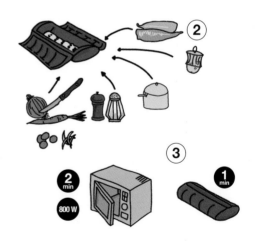

Tips and tricks

- *Vegetables will be "al dente", but if you like them more cooked, you can leave it to cook for 1 more minute before adding the fish and then follow the same steps.*
- *You can use other kinds of fish such as sea bass, gilthead sea bream, or mackerel.*
- *You can use whatever different vegetables you have in the fridge.*

Fish

Provençal Striped Bass

Ingredients

- 🍅 **1 medium** tomato, chopped
- 🧅 **1/4 cup** yellow onion, chopped
- 🥤 **1 tbsp** water
- 🫙 **1 tbsp** olive oil
- 🧄 **1 clove** of garlic

- 🧂 Salt
- Sugar
- 🌿 Rosemary
- 🫙 Pepper
- 🐟 **1 - 5 oz fillet** of striped bass

Directions

❶ Put the onion, water, oil, garlic, and a pinch of salt and pepper into the Lékué Steam Case. Cook for 2 minutes at 800 watts.

❷ Add the chopped tomato to the Lékué Steam Case along with the rosemary, pinch of sugar and pinch of salt. Cook for 4 minutes at 800 watts.

❸ Add the bass to the Lékué Steam Case on top of the tomato mixture. Season with salt and pepper. Cook in the microwave for 1 minute and 30 seconds at 800 watts and let sit for 1 more minute before opening the steam case.

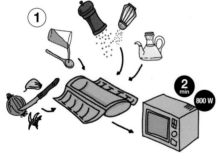

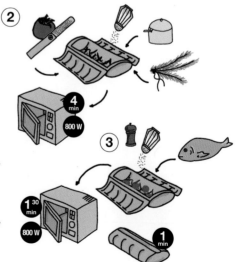

Tips and tricks

- *Sprinkle fish with virgin olive oil just before eating for added flavor.*
- *Give it a different taste by adding green or black olives.*
- *The best condiment for this dish is, of course, Provençal-style herbs!*
- *If you're short on time, you can use canned crushed tomato, but never tomato frito!*

Steamed Garlic Shrimp

Ingredients

 5 - 6 peeled shrimp

 Salt

 2 tbsp water

Pepper

1 tbsp olive oil

1 clove of garlic

Directions

❶ Put the tray in the Lékué Steam Case. Put the water in the case.

❷ Place the shrimp in a bowl and coat with the olive oil, garlic, salt and pepper. Place the coated shrimp in the case. Close the lids and cook in the microwave for 2 minutes and 30 seconds at 800 watts.

❸ Remove the case from the microwave and let sit with the lids closed for about 30 seconds.

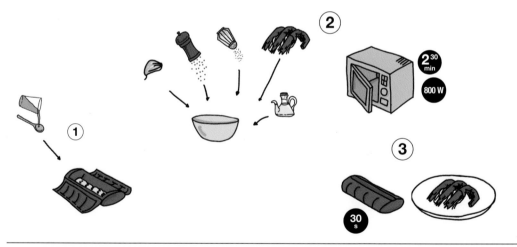

Tips and tricks

- You can also serve them with sauces such as mayonnaise, alioli, spicy tomato sauce or cocktail sauce.
- Shellfish are an excellent source of vitamins (B1, B12) and minerals such as phosphorus, potassium, iron, iodine, fluoride and zinc. They are rich in proteins and low in sodium, calories and saturated fats.
- You can add some aromatic ingredients under the tray such as bay leaves, pepper, lemon or orange peels or a stick of rosemary.

Salmon with Cayenne and Paprika

Ingredients

 1 - 5 oz Salmon medallion

 5 tbsp oil

 1 clove of garlic

 1 tsp cayenne pepper

 1 tsp paprika

 Salt and pepper

Directions

❶ Put the oil, chopped garlic, and cayenne pepper into the Lékué Steam Case.

❷ Add the salmon and sprinkle with salt and pepper. Cook for 2 minutes at 800 watts.

❸ Let sit for an additional minute with the lids closed. Remove the salmon from the Lekue Steam Case and put on a plate. Then add the paprika and oil to the case and blend together with the other ingredients. Pour the sauce over the salmon before serving.

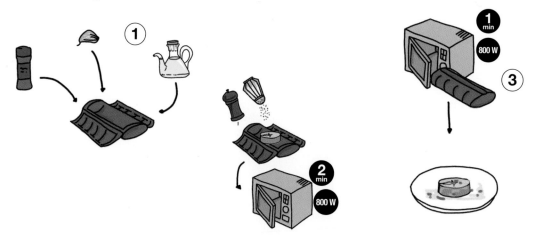

Tips and tricks

- Leave the cayenne pepper out if you don't like spicy food.
- To make it more authentic, add a bit of vinegar at the beginning with the oil, garlic and cayenne pepper.
- Cooking times for salmon may vary according to their cut. A thick slice of about 1.5 in. (4 cm) would be the ideal cut.
- Serve this dish along with a microwaved potato. See initial cooking tables.

Fish

Sea Bass with Vegetables

Ingredients

 2 tsp water

 1 - 5 oz fillet sea bass

Salt

 Pepper

 1 small carrot

 1/2 medium zucchini

Directions

❶ Put water in the Lékué Steam Case and then add the tray. Place the sea bass on the tray and season with a pinch of salt and pepper.

❷ Cut the vegetables into slices and place them on top of the fish. Season again with a pinch of salt and pepper. Close the lids and cook in the microwave for 2 minutes at 800 watts.

❸ Let sit for an additional minute before opening the lids.

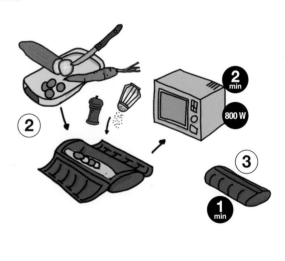

Tips and tricks

- If you want the vegetables to be a little more cooked, you can cook them first for 2 minutes on the rack with two tablespoons of water.
- You can add raw olive oil at the end to enhance its flavor, or you can serve it with a vinaigrette sauce made using 2 parts soy sauce and 1 part sesame oil. You can also sprinkle some toasted almond slices or pistachios on top to give it a bit of a crunch.
- Serving suggestion: When serving, put a tablespoon of tomato frito with olive oil and, if desired, some herbs such as basil, parsley or thyme right on the plate. Then, just place the fish on top of this base.

Meat

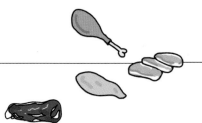

Chicken Parmesan

Ingredients

 3 tbsp crushed tomatoes or fresh chopped tomatoes

 2 slices fresh mozzarella cheese

 Salt and pepper

 1 tbsp olive oil

 2 tbsp water

 2 thin chicken breasts or 1 half boneless, skinless chicken breast cut in half and butterflied open

Directions

❶ Put the water in the bottom of the Lékué Steam Case and then fit the tray inside. Put the chicken breasts on top of the tray. Drizzle the olive oil over the chicken breasts and then season with a pinch of salt and pepper. Close the lids and cook in the microwave for 3 minutes at 800 watts.

❷ Remove from the microwave, spoon the tomatoes on top of the chicken and then place the slice of mozzarella. Season again with a pinch of salt and pepper.

❸ Close the lids again and cook for an additional 1 minute and 30 seconds at 800 watts.

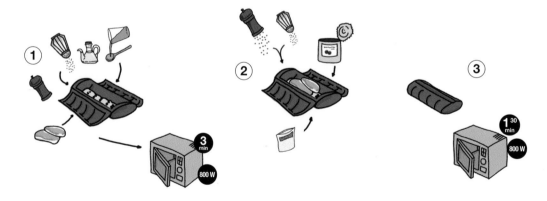

Tips and tricks

- If you don't have crushed tomatoes, you can use fresh sliced tomatoes or even tomato frito.
- You can also add other spices such as basil or oregano.
- To vary this recipe, you can sprinkle some breadcrumbs on top of the cheese.

Meat

Sweet or Spicy Sausage with Vegetables

Ingredients

 1/4 zucchini, cut into sticks

 1 small carrot, cut into sticks

 1/2 small onion, roughly chopped

 1/4 tomato, finely chopped

2 asparagus, halved

 2 mushrooms, sliced

 1 tbsp extra virgin olive oil

 Salt

 2 links sausage

 2 tbsp water

Directions

❶ Cut the vegetables into strips. Add all vegetables to the Lékué Steam Case along with water, oil, and a pinch of salt.

❷ Close the lids and cook in the microwave for 3 minutes and 30 seconds at 800 watts. Remove the casing from the sausages by making a shallow slit on the side. You will be able to peel it off easily. Cut the sausage into bite size pieces. Add the sausage to the steam case, close the lids and cook for another 2 minutes and 30 seconds.

❸ Remove from the microwave and enjoy.

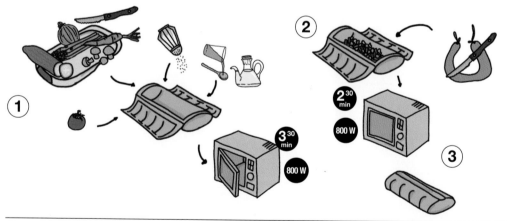

Tips and tricks

- You can season this dish with tomato sauce, garlic oil and parsley.
- You can add mushrooms such as oyster, button, or shiitake mushrooms, if desired.

Chicken Breasts with Honey Mustard

Ingredients

🐟 **1** carrot

🥛 **2 tbsp** water

🧂 Salt and pepper

🍗 **1** chicken breast

Vinaigrette:

🫗 **3 tbsp** olive oil

🫙 **1 tsp** Dijon mustard

🍯 **1 tsp** honey

Directions

❶ Peel the carrot and cut into sticks. Put the carrot sticks, water, and a pinch of salt into the Lékué Steam Case. Close the lids and cook for 2 minutes.

❷ In a bowl mix the olive oil, honey, and mustard together until combined. Add a pinch of salt and pepper. Butterfly the chicken breast.

❸ Once the carrots are finished, put the chicken breast into the case and pour the vinaigrette on top. Close the lids and cook for another 3 minutes. Let sit for 30 seconds with the lids closed.

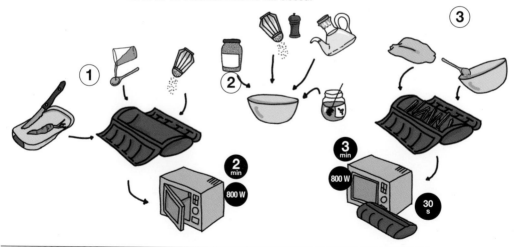

Tips and tricks

- You can also use turkey fillets.
- You can complete the dish by adding slivers of toasted peanuts on top.

Meat

Beef Strips with Tomato and Onion

Ingredients

 1/2 cup steak strips

 1 small yellow onion

 1 medium tomato

 2 tbsp olive oil

 2 tbsp soy sauce

 Pepper

 Salt - to taste

Directions

❶ Chop the tomato and thinly slice the onion. Put everything (except salt) into the Lékué Steam Case.

❷ Cook in the microwave for 2 minutes and 30 seconds at 800 watts.

❸ Let sit for 30 seconds before opening lids. Taste the beef and add salt if needed.

 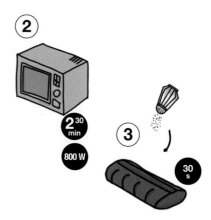

Tips and tricks

- The onion will turn out crunchy, since the vegetables of this dish are supposed to be in wok-style.
- You can correct with salt in the end if it seems too sweet. Given the taste of the soy sauce, we don't add salt at the beginning.
- Serve with fajitas and your meal is complete.
- Delicious when served on small cooked beans or boiled rice. If you're feeling adventurous you can try other grains such as quinoa, millet, etc.

Meat

Marinated Pork Loin

Ingredients

 3 3/4 slices of pork loin

 1 tbsp paprika

 1 pinch of cumin

 1 pinch of oregano

 Salt and pepper

 2 tbsp extra virgin olive oil

Directions

❶ Dice the pork in cubed pieces, place in the Lékué Steam Case and season with salt and pepper.

❷ Add remaining ingredients and blend.

❸ Cook in the microwave for 2 minutes with the lids closed (800 W). Let sit for an additional 30 seconds before opening. Stir well before eating.

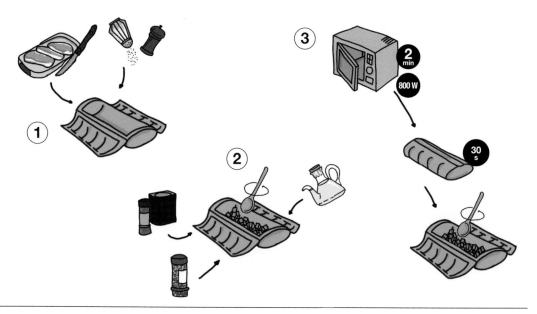

Tips and tricks

- You can serve this dish as skewers as if they were "shish kebabs".
- The amounts of spices can vary according to your taste.

Desserts

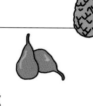

Desserts

Rosemary Pears

Ingredients

 1 small pear

1 sprig fresh rosemary

 2 tbsp water

 1 tbsp sugar

Directions

❶ Dice the pear and place in the Lékué Steam Case.

❷ Add the water, sugar, and rosemary.

❸ Close the lids and cook in the microwave for 3 minutes and 30 seconds at 800 watts. Remove the rosemary and enjoy.

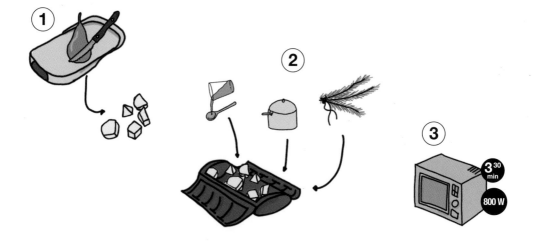

Tips and tricks

- If you can't find fresh rosemary you can use dried rosemary or even cinnamon powder or cardamom.
- It's a good idea to eat fruit with the skin unpeeled, as this is a good source of not only vitamins and minerals, but also fiber.
- Eat this dessert twice a week, and don't replace your daily fruit intake with sugary desserts.
- Try mixing the diced pear with your breakfast cereal, custard or yogurt.
- On special occasions you can serve the pears with whipped cream or melted chocolate, or ice cream.

Whole Wheat Cake with Walnuts

Ingredients

 ¼ cup olive oil or sunflower oil

 ¼ cup sugar

 1 egg

 2 ½ tbsp water

 ¼ cup whole-wheat flour

 1 tsp baking powder

 3 tbsp walnut slivers

Directions

❶ Start adding the ingredients into the Lékué Steam Case one by one in the order they appear above. Each time you add an ingredient, mix well until uniform.

❷ Close the lids and cook at 800 watts for 3 minutes and 30 seconds. When it is done cooking, let it sit for 2 more minutes with the lids open.

❸ To remove from the Lékué Steam Case, make sure the edges aren't sticking by running a butter knife or spatula along the sides. Then, flip the cake over onto a plate.

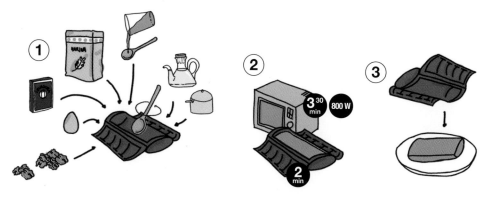

Tips and tricks

- You can use plain wheat flour if you don't have whole-wheat flour.
- You can sprinkle walnuts on top of the cake to decorate.
- You can use sunflower oil instead of olive oil to give it a less intense flavor, or you can use butter (3 1/2 tablespoons, or 50 g) to enhance its flavor. Follow the same steps.
- If you leave it out of the refrigerator for a long time and it gets dried out, you can use it to make coffee pudding (see Lékué recipe on page 76).
- Slice and toast it for breakfast or make a delicious sweet sandwich.

Coffee Pudding

5 min   4

Ingredients

 1 cup milk

 2 eggs

¼ **cup** sugar

2 slices dried/sliced bread

2 espressos

Directions

❶ Add the bread and coffee into the Lékué Steam Case. With a fork, mix together until the bread is broken up well.

❷ In a separate bowl mix together the milk, eggs, and sugar until homogenous. Add this mixture to the case and cook for 5 minutes at 800 watts.

❸ To remove the pudding, flip the case over onto a plate.

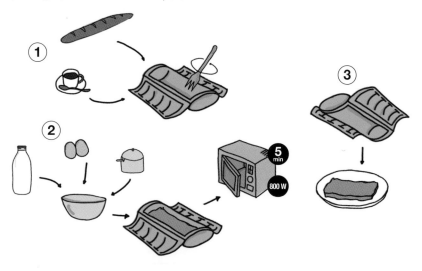

Tips and tricks

- If you don't like coffee, simply don't put any of it in the dish and you'll still make an excellent pudding.
- Flavor your pudding with cinnamon, lemon peels or vanilla.
- Serve the coffee pudding with whipped cream and rosemary pears (page 72).
- If desired, you can make it with pieces of sponge cake, cupcakes or cookies.

4 min · 1

Roast Pineapple with Yogurt

Ingredients

 3.5 oz plain pineapple (1 slice)

 1 yogurt

 Cinnamon

Nutmeg

Black pepper

Directions

❶ Cut pineapple into three pieces and place in the Lékué Steam Case.

❷ Cook for 4 minutes (800 W).

❸ Serve on a plate of yogurt, add pineapple on top and sprinkle different spices on each piece.

Tips and tricks

- You can decorate the dish with some toasted cashews to give it a bit of a crunch.
- You can choose to cook the pineapple and add it straight to yogurt flavored with sugar and a bit of black pepper.
- Another option would be to decorate the dish with a banana and sprinkle it with some spices.
- You can mix the yogurt with grated coconut instead of spices to make a "piña colada" dessert.